RAINFOREST ANIMALS FOR KIDS
Wild Habitats Facts, Photos and Fun
Children's Environment Books Edition

SPEEDY
PUBLISHING

Rainforests are tremendously
rich in animal life.

The tiger is the
biggest species
of the cat family.
Each tiger has
a unique set
of stripes.

Most Tigers live in Asia, specifically throughout Southeast Asia, China, Korea and Russia. They live in a variety of habitats from tropical rain forests to mangrove swamps.

The jaguar is the
third-largest cat
after the tiger and
the lion. Jaguars
are nocturnal.
They lounge around
during the day
and hunt at night.

Jaguars are only found in the Americas. The jaguar will range across a variety of forested and open terrains.

Boa Constrictors are one of the largest snakes in the world. Body of boa constrictor can be tan, yellow, red, pinkish or green in color.

Boa constrictors live in Central and South America. They live in variety of habitats: tropical rainforests, savannas and areas near human settlements.

Sloths are a medium-sized mammal characterized by slow movement in the trees. Sloth usually spends 20 hours per day in sleeping.

Sloths are found in Central and South America. They prefer life in dense tropical and subtropical rainforests.

Orangutans have thin, shaggy, reddish-brown hair. Most orangutans are four to five feet long, some can reach a length of six feet.

Orangutans live in Indonesia and Malaysia on the islands of Sumatra and Borneo. Orangutans are arboreal creatures, which means they spend most of their lives slowly walking, swinging and climbing through dense rain forests.

The harpy eagle is one of the largest eagles in the world. Harpy Eagles are carnivores and are the apex predators in their environment.

Harpy eagle inhabits all throughout Mexico, ranging from Central America to the South America and stretching towards Argentina. These birds like to live in the large expanse such as tropical forests.

The scarlet macaw is one of the most beautiful members of the parrot family. Macaws are intelligent and curious birds that like to explore and keep busy.

Scarlet macaw is native to humid evergreen forests of tropical South America.

Poison dart frogs
are one of the
most brightly-
colored creatures
on the planet.
Poison frogs are
known to eat
ants, termites,
and beetles.

Poison Dart frogs
are endemic to
tropical Central
and South America.
They can be found
in trees, as well
as under leaves
and logs and rocks
on the floor of
the forest.

Leafcutter ants form the largest and most complex animal societies on Earth. These ants consume more vegetation than any other animal group.

They are all
endemic to South
and Central
America, Mexico,
and parts of
the southern
United States.